DEFIANCE

BOOKS BY JOHN PATRICK SHANLEY
AVAILABLE FROM TCG

Defiance

Dirty Story and Other Plays
INCLUDES:
Dirty Story
Where's My Money?
Sailor's Song

Doubt
(A Parable)

DEFIANCE

John Patrick Shanley

THEATRE COMMUNICATIONS GROUP
NEW YORK
2007

Defiance is published by Theatre Communications Group, Inc.,
520 Eighth Avenue, 24th Floor, New York, NY 10018-4156

This publication is made possible in part with public funds from
the New York State Council on the Arts, a State Agency.

TCG books are exclusively distributed to the book trade by Consortium Book
Sales and Distribution, 1045 Westgate Drive, St. Paul, MN 55114.

LIBRARY OF CONGRESS CATALOGING-IN-PUBLICATION DATA
Shanley, John Patrick.
Defiance / by John Patrick Shanley.—1st ed.
p. cm.
ISBN 978-1-55936-309-9
1. Marines—United States—Drama. 2. Camp Lejeune (N.C.) —History—
20th century—Drama. 3. North Carolina—Race relations—Drama. I. Title.
PS3569.H3337D44 2007
812'.54—dc22 2007035058

Cover design by John Gall
Cover photo by Ryan McVay/Getty Images
Author photo by Monique Carboni
Text design and composition by Lisa Govan

First Edition, November 2007

This play is dedicated to August Wilson,
a great American playwright

DEFIANCE

PRODUCTION HISTORY

Defiance was originally produced by the Manhattan Theatre Club (Lynne Meadow, Artistic Director; Barry Grove, Executive Producer) in New York City, opening on February 9, 2006. It was directed by Doug Hughes; the set design was by John Lee Beatty, the costume design was by Catherine Zuber, the lighting design was by Pat Collins, the original music and sound design were by David Van Tieghem; the production stage manager was James Fitzsimmons. The cast was as follows:

LIEUTENANT COLONEL	
MORGAN LITTLEFIELD	Stephen Lang
MARGARET LITTLEFIELD	Magaret Colin
CAPTAIN LEE KING	Chris Chalk
CHAPLAIN WHITE	Chris Bauer
GUNNEY SERGEANT	Trevor Long
PRIVATE FIRST CLASS EVAN DAVIS	Jeremy Strong

CHARACTERS

Lieutenant Colonel Morgan Littlefield
Margaret Littlefield
Captain Lee King
Chaplain White
Gunney Sergeant
Private First Class Evan Davis

TIME

Spring 1971

PLACE

Camp Lejeune, North Carolina

Herein lies the tragedy of the age: not that men are poor—all men know something of poverty; not that men are wicked—who is good? Not that men are ignorant—what is Truth? Nay, but that men know so little of men.

—W.E.B. DU BOIS

We are the same people, only further from home.

—LAWRENCE FERLINGHETTI

SCENE 1

Camp Lejeune, North Carolina, spring 1971. We're in front of the unseen H&S Company barracks. The Gunney Sergeant, twenty-eight but looks thirty-five, comes out and walks downstage. He surveys the platoon/audience. He's in sweat-stained utilities, mud-splashed boots, wearing a haversack and shelter half, carrying an M16. He's disgusted. He doesn't speak too loudly, not wanting to be overheard by the brass. He's a lifer from Florida.

GUNNEY: A marine will be in jail tonight because he asked me a question. I gave him the lawful order to mount up and he asked me, "Why?" That was the cherry on the cake for me. Eighteen years I have been in the corps and that was the goddamn cherry on the cake. This is the most sorry unsquared-away field exercise I have participated in for the term of my enlistment, gentlemen. *(Points)* Get up, Conroy! *(Reacts to a comment)* I don't care if your leg's broke. *(Another man gets his attention)* You got somethin' to say,

Lance Corporal Wiggins? 'Cause I WILL have you put inside the fence. Correctional Custody is doing bookoo business today courtesy of Headquarters & Service Company. Two men so far. And the day ain't done yet. *(Sound of a very distant Lieutenant Colonel makes him look)*

LIEUTENANT COLONEL *(Offstage)*: Stand by!

GUNNEY: Now that's the goddamn battalion commander, you understand? Get ready to look like marines or I WILL have you busted down to basic insignificant subatomic particles. Stand by.

(The Gunney Sergeant walks smartly to the side, turns away from us, assumes the parade rest position, legs apart, hands clasped behind. Four offstage Sergeants at different distances cry out in turn:)

SERGEANT 1 *(Offstage)*: Platoon!

SERGEANT 2 *(Offstage)*: Platoon!

SERGEANT 3 *(Offstage)*: Platoon!

SERGEANT 4 *(Offstage)*: Platoon!

GUNNEY: Company!

(A Captain can be heard in the distance:)

CAPTAIN *(Offstage)*: Battalion!

GUNNEY AND OFFSTAGE VOICES: 'TENTION!

(The Gunney Sergeant snaps to attention, saluting. Lieutenant Colonel Morgan Littlefield enters. He's around fifty, wears the insignia of his rank: the silver oak leaf, on the collar of his slightly sweaty but perfectly starched utilities. He's from Maryland. He's tough, intelligent, well educated, private. He returns the Gunney Sergeant's salute.)

GUNNEY: All present and accounted for, sir!

(Littlefield looks over the unseen troops. He comments unfavorably and publicly on one man after another:)

LITTLEFIELD: You. You're at attention, Marine. How 'bout getting those feet at a forty-five-degree angle? Unbloused boot. Is that a standard issue T-shirt, Private? I don't think so. Halfway to a goddamn turtleneck. I see it again, it will cost you. You. With the vomit. Fall out and see the corpsman. *(More generally)* This company is a disgrace to the Sixth Marines. You are not combat ready. You do not have your shit together. I do not like you. Now hear this. There were two racial incidents during the course of these ten days in the field. I WILL NOT COUNTENANCE RACIAL INCIDENTS IN MY BATTALION! Not in my wigwam! Do you understand? The five marines responsible for these incidents face a general court. They WILL go to jail. We are having an attitude problem, gentlemen. Due to some bad apples. Fully one-third of this battalion is composed of men who have returned from service in Vietnam. I want you to know. I don't care. It don't make you special. I don't care if you don't know why you're still in uniform. I don't care how short you are. You will stand tall or you will pay the price. And as for this racial nonsense, it matters to me not at all if you're black, white, blue or stupid. You are marines. You are green in the eyes of the corps. And you will meet the standard of the corps. Or get eighty-sixed. Liberty for this weekend is suspended. Company commanders will carry out squadbay inspections followed by junk-on-the-bunk inspections of all barracks on Saturday at sixteen-hundred hours. And then I will be walking through! Troops will be dismissed by company. Gunney!

GUNNEY: Yes, sir!

LITTLEFIELD: Get these men to work!

GUNNEY: Yes, sir!

(*Littlefield strides off. The Gunney Sergeant faces his troops.*)

Fall out!

(*The lights fade.*)

SCENE 2

The Littlefield home. It's officers' housing. We're in the living room. There's a foyer off right, and bit of kitchen off left. It's a clean, generic place made hospitable with flowers and books. At the lights come up, Margaret Littlefield is setting the coffee table for tea. The tea set is warm and personal. Margaret, in her early forties, wears a sundress. She's attractive, from a good Florida family. A wall phone rings. She answers it.

MARGARET: Hello? Hey, Skipper, where are you? You're *still* talking to the chaplain? Why don't you let that poor man alone! (*Listens briefly*) I've been home for forty minutes. No. (*Listens briefly*) Morgan, it's Sunday, the day of *rest*? (*The doorbell rings*) The doorbell just rang. Probably. Well, hurry up then! (*Hangs up the phone as the doorbell rings again*) On the way!

(*She goes off right. She lets someone in. We hear her and a guest, offstage:*)

Good morning, Captain.

CAPTAIN KING (*Offstage*): Good morning, ma'am.

MARGARET (Offstage): Colonel Littlefield isn't back from services yet, but come on in.

(They enter. Captain Lee King is twenty-seven, from Washington, DC. He's a serious, reserved, physically powerful man who's worked hard all his life. He's wearing the uniform of the day [UD], khakis. He holds his hat under his arm.)

May I take your cover?

(He hands his hat to her.)

CAPTAIN KING: Thank you, ma'am.
MARGARET: Have a seat.

(He sits down. He's not insecure, but he'd rather be someplace else. Margaret sees this, and doesn't mind. She's used to the military.)

CAPTAIN KING: Thank you.
MARGARET: Would you like a glass of water till Morgan gets here?
CAPTAIN KING: No, thank you.
MARGARET: He'll be here in a minute. How long you been stationed at Camp Lejeune?
CAPTAIN KING: Eighteen months. Mostly with Second Battalion.
MARGARET: And before that?
CAPTAIN KING: Vietnam.
MARGARET: Married?
CAPTAIN KING: No, ma'am.
MARGARET: How many tours in Vietnam?
CAPTAIN KING: Two.
MARGARET: Did Morgan tell me you have a law degree?
CAPTAIN KING: I've been serving as a judge advocate on both sides of the table for the last year. Court martials. Just

sort've fell into it. I don't have a law degree. Corps doesn't require it. Just a good knowledge of the Uniform Code of Military Justice.

MARGARET: Business been good?

CAPTAIN KING: Too darn good. That's why I'm here. Camp's in bad shape. Colonel wants answers. Not that I have any.

MARGARET: You're a mustanger, aren't you?

CAPTAIN KING: Yes, ma'am.

MARGARET: So was Morgan. Always admire that. Up from the ranks.

CAPTAIN KING: If the offer still stands, I would take a glass of water, ma'am.

MARGARET (*Sets about doing that*): Good. Actually, I have lemonade.

CAPTAIN KING: Water's fine.

MARGARET: I'd have poured you coffee, but I'm waiting till the Skipper comes to pull out the big guns. Sorry he's not here. After the church service the . . . You weren't at the service, were you, Captain?

CAPTAIN KING: No.

MARGARET: Morgan started in talking to the new chaplain . . . Have you met him?

CAPTAIN KING: No, ma'am.

MARGARET: His name is White.

CAPTAIN KING: I've seen it posted.

MARGARET: He's Lutheran. Tell me again, what do the Lutherans believe?

CAPTAIN KING: That they're not Catholics.

MARGARET: Very good! I do believe you have just summarized every Protestant religion.

CAPTAIN KING: Yes, ma'am.

MARGARET: He seems nice, the chaplain, met him this morning. Morgan's trying to instill something in the fellow. I'm not sure what. Anyway, that's why he's late. I'm sure there's something you'd rather be doing. (*No answer*) Talking to the

CO's wife on Sunday. *(No answer)* You watch football?

CAPTAIN KING: I do not.

MARGARET: You're better off. I follow it to have something in common with my son. Oh look at that. Excuse me. His picture's fallen over. *(Goes to a side table and stands the photo up again)* That's better.

CAPTAIN KING: Nice face. What's his name?

MARGARET: Joe. I'm reading a book. Very interesting. Do you read much?

CAPTAIN KING: I read.

MARGARET: It's called *Future Shock*. Have you heard of it?

CAPTAIN KING: Sure. It's a bestseller.

MARGARET: It describes the future as something that's hitting us like a truck.

(King smiles.)

CAPTAIN KING: All right.

MARGARET: What's funny?

CAPTAIN KING: I don't know. The future hasn't done anything to me.

MARGARET: Wait a while.

(The doorbell rings. She goes to answer it.)

Now who's this and where's Morgan?

(She's out of view, opening the door; offstage:)

Well, Chaplain! How you doing?

CHAPLAIN *(Offstage)*: Excellent!

MARGARET *(Offstage)*: Lovely service, by the way.

CHAPLAIN *(Offstage)*: You're very kind! Thank you, Mrs. Littlefield.

13

MARGARET (*Offstage*): Please call me Meg. Where's Morgan?

CHAPLAIN (*Offstage*): Right there. He's just talking to his driver.

MARGARET (*Offstage*): Oh, him and that driver. That man's going to be his ruin. Well, let's not wait on him! Come in!

(*Margaret enters with Chaplain White, also in UDs. He's thirty-five, a First Lieutenant, Junior Grade, wearing a naval uniform. He's from Alabama.*)

Do you know Captain King?

CHAPLAIN: No, this is our first encounter. I'm new to base. How d'you do, Captain King, a real pleasure.

CAPTAIN KING: Nice to meet you, Chaplain.

CHAPLAIN: Just gave my first sermon.

CAPTAIN KING: Congratulations.

MARGARET: It was lovely.

CHAPLAIN: Went over like a lead balloon.

MARGARET: It did not!

CHAPLAIN: Next week'll be better. I will ingratiate myself. (*To King*) Did I see you at services today?

CAPTAIN KING: No.

CHAPLAIN: You go elsewhere?

CAPTAIN KING: I don't go.

CHAPLAIN: I'm surprised. Usually a man with combat ribbons takes Sunday seriously.

MARGARET: Would you like some lemonade, Chaplain?

CHAPLAIN: I certainly would. Mind if I sit?

MARGARET: Please. (*Goes off to kitchen*)

CHAPLAIN: Well, isn't this nice? Invited to the CO's residence. (*No answer from King*) I'm from Alabama. You?

CAPTAIN KING: DC.

CHAPLAIN: What part?

CAPTAIN KING: Do you know DC?

CHAPLAIN: No.

CAPTAIN KING: Downtown.

CHAPLAIN: Where's that in relation to the White House?

CAPTAIN KING: You can't get there from there.

CHAPLAIN: Oh, I get it! You're giving it to me, aren't you? *(Laughs)* That was a remark. Good for you! You oughta come by next week. Might enjoy it.

(Colonel Littlefield enters. He's in UDs as well. The men stand.)

LITTLEFIELD: I tell you, that driver would lay down *beside* work! Meg, I'm home!

CAPTAIN KING: Good morning, Colonel.

MARGARET *(Off, from kitchen)*: Hi, Skip!

LITTLEFIELD: Good morning, Captain King. I've invited the chaplain to join us. Hope you don't mind. Sit down. Both of you. Just let me take a minute and kiss my wife.

(He meets Margaret as she comes out with the lemonade. He takes the lemonade, kisses her, drinks.)

Hi.

MARGARET: Morgan? Morgan? Morgan.

LITTLEFIELD: Delicious!

MARGARET: You just drank the chaplain's lemonade.

LITTLEFIELD: It was good too. Thanks, Chaplain.

CHAPLAIN: You're very welcome.

MARGARET: I'll get you another.

CHAPLAIN: Don't put yourself out.

MARGARET: I made a batch. *(Heads back into the kitchen)*

CHAPLAIN: You've got quite a treasure there.

(Littlefield blinks at the Chaplain.)

LITTLEFIELD: Duly noted.

(Margaret sticks her head in.)

MARGARET: I'd just like to say one thing, Morgan.
LITTLEFIELD: What?
MARGARET: It's Sunday.

(Disappears back into the kitchen as Littlefield calls after her:)

LITTLEFIELD: Thank you! I thought it was Tuesday and I was in France! You married, Captain?
CAPTAIN KING: No, sir.
LITTLEFIELD: Didn't think so. You look too composed. Well, to the matter at hand. I had asked Captain King over to discuss the state of the battalion and it occurred to me, Chaplain, during your sermon, that you might benefit from sitting in.
CHAPLAIN: I'm delighted to be included.
LITTLEFIELD: Let me start by saying, your sermon was egregious.
CHAPLAIN: I know I didn't . . .
LITTLEFIELD: You can't talk like that to these men. They'll think you're an imbecile.
CHAPLAIN: All right.
LITTLEFIELD: We've got a huge morale problem on this base, and you're talking to these men like they're champing at the bit to die for their country just misses the boat. Captain King.
CAPTAIN KING: Yes, Colonel.
LITTLEFIELD: We need to paint the chaplain a picture.
CAPTAIN KING: Yes, sir.
LITTLEFIELD: Captain King here's on the front line with an increasingly brazen and contemptuous element disrupting this camp. He's been serving as judge advocate, fielding court-martials. What's your backlog, Captain?

CAPTAIN KING: Four months?

LITTLEFIELD: Jesus. We're throwing so many men in the brig, it's starting to look like there's two marine corps.

CHAPLAIN: I had no conception.

LITTLEFIELD: That's why I want you to hear. I want you to understand. It's bad. Built a new brig to replace the old brig, now both are full.

CHAPLAIN: Well, what's the cause?

LITTLEFIELD: Two things. First, half the men rotating back from combat at this point are just sludge in the pipe. Am I right, Captain?

CAPTAIN KING: Lot of drug problems. Resentment.

CHAPLAIN: Why don't you just send 'em home?

LITTLEFIELD: Pentagon. They want the strength levels to look right. Second problem's the new recruits. War's gone on too long. The recruiters are bottom-fishing, sending us riff-raff, hooligans and worse.

CHAPLAIN: What about the baby boom? Isn't the country bursting with fine young men?!

LITTLEFIELD: They don't want to serve.

CHAPLAIN: Why not?

LITTLEFIELD: You got me. Captain?

CAPTAIN KING: They might get killed?

CHAPLAIN: You mean they're cowards?

(This hits Littlefield.)

LITTLEFIELD: Maybe. I don't know.

CHAPLAIN: Be careful. Cynicism's a pitfall. It excuses wrong-doing even before wrong is done.

LITTLEFIELD: I hope you're not one of those fellas that's got a little maxim for every occasion, padre. Anyway, the end result of what I've been describing is: We've got one heck of a racial problem here at Camp Lejeune.

(Margaret enters with lemonade and three glasses. The men stand for her.)

What have *you* got for us, Meg?

MARGARET: More lemonade.

LITTLEFIELD: How much lemonade can a man drink?

MARGARET: Wake up. You're the only one who's had any.

LITTLEFIELD: Put me in my place.

MARGARET: It's there for who wants it. I'll have coffee up in a minute.

(Margaret exits again.)

CHAPLAIN: Thank you, Mrs. Littlefield. *(Offering to pour)* Colonel?

LITTLEFIELD: I'm good.

CHAPLAIN: I'll have a drop. Looks so cold! I can't resist a cold drink. *(Serves himself)* Captain?

CAPTAIN KING: No, thank you.

LITTLEFIELD: Have some.

CAPTAIN KING: Sure.

CHAPLAIN *(Pouring lemonade)*: I'm sorry to hear the camp's in such an unruly state. But I enjoy a challenge. Certainly you want to take action. But a disputatious man is like a knife that's fallen in the tall grass. You got to take a minute, locate the handle first, grab it right. You gotta take that extra minute.

(A smudge of silence. The Chaplain notices the photo.)

Is that fine-looking young man your son?

LITTLEFIELD: Never mind that.

(Littlefield goes over to the photo. He puts it facedown on the table.)

My son's gone to Canada.

CHAPLAIN: Oh.

LITTLEFIELD: Bolted. Last week.

CHAPLAIN: My goodness.

LITTLEFIELD: Where was I?

CAPTAIN KING: Racial problem.

LITTLEFIELD: Right. Would you agree?

CAPTAIN KING: Yes, sir.

LITTLEFIELD: Had a race riot before I got here. Damn near had another a few months ago. Murders, too.

CHAPLAIN: Murder!

LITTLEFIELD: Oh yes. Mostly in town, in Jacksonville. We just had an incendiary case of rape last week. A black marine raped a white marine right here on base.

CHAPLAIN: What d'you mean? Are we talking about men?

LITTLEFIELD: Yes.

CHAPLAIN: I can't even imagine that. Literally.

LITTLEFIELD: Well, I'm not going to help you. You know how the fool got caught? Took the wrong pants, left his wallet. This is what you're going to be facing, Chaplain. Criminal idiocy. So the next time you preach, I strongly suggest you aim low.

CHAPLAIN: I hear you, but I think I can be of more help than that, Colonel!

LITTLEFIELD: How?

CHAPLAIN: Seems to me I should not pander. Seems to me I should point out the path upward, towards a target in the sky! A sparkling ideal!

LITTLEFIELD: No, you should not.

CHAPLAIN: In a plan of battle, shouldn't the objective be victory?

LITTLEFIELD: I will provide leadership. You will provide consolation. Understood?

CHAPLAIN: Yes, sir.

LITTLEFIELD: Good. Any thoughts before I move on to Captain King?

CHAPLAIN: Well. *(Soft-pedaling)* What these men need to understand is life is more enjoyable when you do good things rather than bad things. Good things pile up just like bad things except what you end up with is good. What I would like to do, through my service, is remind them of that.

LITTLEFIELD: That's your best shot?

CHAPLAIN: Excuse me?

LITTLEFIELD: What if they don't come to your service?

CHAPLAIN: Maybe you could encourage the men to attend?

LITTLEFIELD: I don't believe in that. Man wants church, it's his business. Doesn't want it, that's fine too.

CHAPLAIN: Colonel, I believe I can invigorate the troops if they see you're behind me.

LITTLEFIELD: If anybody's going to be behind anybody, Chaplain White, you're going to be behind me.

CHAPLAIN: The more I'm identified with command, the more moral authority you will have.

LITTLEFIELD: My authority is not at issue.

CHAPLAIN: Well, I'd just like to observe. Sometimes a morale problem is really a morality problem.

LITTLEFIELD: That has a nice ring to it, but I'm not sure it means much. You should probably know, Chaplain, that I don't believe in anything much but my wife's cooking.

So, Captain King, the camp has a racial problem.

CAPTAIN KING: Yes, sir.

LITTLEFIELD: What's to be done?

CAPTAIN KING: I don't know.

LITTLEFIELD: You have thoughts about it?

CAPTAIN KING: No, sir.

LITTLEFIELD: Come on, Captain. I want to know what you think. That's why I invited you over.

CAPTAIN KING: Why?

LITTLEFIELD: 'Cause I'm gonna have to intervene here, and I'm trying to figure out the nature of the intervention.

CAPTAIN KING: I'm no expert.

LITTLEFIELD: You're . . . All right, all right. Let's just chat. Gimme half a glass of that lemonade, Chaplain.

CHAPLAIN: Glad to oblige. *(Pours)*

LITTLEFIELD: There's a practice among black marines that I find disturbing. *(To the Chaplain, regarding lemonade)* Stop there. A half I said. Have you seen this handshake the black marines do? It's all over camp. They sort've punch around each other's fist?

CHAPLAIN *(Simultaneously)*: No.

CAPTAIN KING *(Simultaneously)*: Yes.

LITTLEFIELD: They call it giving each other the Power. They're talking about Black Power. And they're doing this in uniform.

CHAPLAIN: Well, now if I may say, that is definitely not right. There's only one Power and it don't have a color. I've listened to these black leaders talk about Black Power. It's seditious. There's no place for it in the armed services. I don't think there's any place for it in the United States!

LITTLEFIELD: I want to hear from Captain King. *(To King)* I'm also hearing from my staff NCOs that black marines are systematically cutting into the mess line, intimidating and challenging the white marines. It's explosive.

(Margaret comes out with coffee and three danishes. They all stand until she sits.)

MARGARET: Coffee's ready.

LITTLEFIELD: Oh, thanks, Meg. Smells good. Anything smell better than coffee? Well, what do you think's going on, Captain?

CAPTAIN KING: I don't have thoughts on the subject.

CHAPLAIN: Well, I do. Black Power is wrongheaded. It's about raising up one man over another. How do you take your coffee, Captain?

CAPTAIN KING: Black.

CHAPLAIN: Black it is! We need a unity in purpose. Like my father used to say: "We all need to be singing the same hymn."

LITTLEFIELD: I agree with you there. A battalion has to answer an order like one man. One man or you're all dead. There are many ways to divide troops and all of them are bad. It can start with small things. I've been told that many black marines are insisting that they shave with butter knives.

CHAPLAIN: Is that possible?

MARGARET: A butter knife? *(Looks at King for confirmation)*

CAPTAIN KING: Many black men have an allergic reaction to shaving with a razor blade.

CHAPLAIN: What do you mean? What kind of reaction?

CAPTAIN KING: Bumps. They get bumps on their skin. So they have to apply a chemical that loosens the facial hair and then scrape it off with a butter knife.

CHAPLAIN: What kind of chemical?

CAPTAIN KING: It's a product called Magic Shaver.

MARGARET: Black marines use Magic Shaver?

CAPTAIN KING: Many of them.

MARGARET: I use Magic Shaver! On my legs.

LITTLEFIELD: Never mind your legs! Let's not wander. My point is our black marines seem to be setting themselves apart and it's no good.

MARGARET: It smells awful. Magic Shaver. I went back to shaving cream.

LITTLEFIELD: Meg?

MARGARET: Sorry.

CAPTAIN KING: It does smell bad. I went back to shaving cream, too.

LITTLEFIELD: So even you have used this alternative method of shaving, Captain?

CAPTAIN KING: I get the bumps. I have black skin.

CHAPLAIN: I don't care what color a man is myself. I just don't even look to see. There are those who say Jesus Christ may have been black. *(To King)* Or at least swarthy.

What do you think of this Black Power?

CAPTAIN KING: Just words.

LITTLEFIELD: You don't think there's a racial problem on the base?

CAPTAIN KING: Oh, I know there's a racial problem, but it isn't because of Black Power.

LITTLEFIELD: It isn't?

CAPTAIN KING: No, sir.

LITTLEFIELD: Then what?

CAPTAIN KING: It's because there isn't any *black power*. *(Pause)* On base or off.

LITTLEFIELD: I don't care about what happens off the base.

CAPTAIN KING: What's going on out there is the root of what's going on in here.

LITTLEFIELD *(Lambasting King)*: I don't accept that! We're a world apart, Captain! Let me tell you something. I was raised in a cheap attached house in suburban Baltimore. I heard more racial filth out of my father's ignorant mouth than I can stomach to remember. I was ashamed of my own. I joined the corps to escape that shame and fight in clearly demarcated fights on the side of Right. Support what's best. Be able to stand proud. Now I don't mind a scuffle and I've been in some. But not with my own! I consider every marine my brother in arms and I stand with my brothers. And I will not allow ideas of injustice out there to justify wrong behavior in here!

MARGARET: More coffee?

LITTLEFIELD: No. Thank you.

CHAPLAIN: May I commend what you just said, Colonel. It is eloquent, and to the point. Black Power is completely unacceptable to the military.

CAPTAIN KING: Why?

CHAPLAIN: Captain?

CAPTAIN KING: You know what Black Power's against?

CHAPLAIN: I'd say white people.

CAPTAIN KING: No. Black Power's against a black man. Martin Luther King to be exact. Martin Luther King was preaching nonviolence. And some black men said no: we want to fight for what's ours. Now if you want to talk about a philosophy that doesn't work for the military, I would think Dr. King's nonviolence is your man. At least Black Power condones the spirit of aggression. That's something we can work with. We are trying to make warriors here, after all, aren't we?

CHAPLAIN (Laughs uneasily): I just don't know what you're going to say next.

(Littlefield stands abruptly.)

LITTLEFIELD: Chaplain!

CHAPLAIN: Yes, Colonel?

LITTLEFIELD: I want to thank you for dropping by.

CHAPLAIN: Oh yes. Well I . . .

LITTLEFIELD: You stay, Captain.

(The Chaplain is humiliated.)

CHAPLAIN: Ah. Well. Thank you, Mrs. Littlefield.

MARGARET: Here's your cover, Chaplain. Take a bun with you.

CHAPLAIN: Thank you. I'll enjoy it after lunch. Nice to see you, Colonel. Captain King.

CAPTAIN KING: Chaplain.

CHAPLAIN (To King): Consider coming to services.

LITTLEFIELD (Showing the Chaplain out): Very good, Chaplain. We'll be talking. Have my driver take you home. Don't be afraid to wake him up. Good. Good.

(Littlefield returns.)

Next week we're going to the Episcopal service.

MARGARET: Well, you invited his opinion.

LITTLEFIELD: My mistake. I suppose he'll do. Last chaplain we had was a fine officer. Good sounding board. Captain, I'm sorry I lit off on you.

CAPTAIN KING: No problem, sir.

LITTLEFIELD: I'm frustrated. I want to take action and I can't get a clear bite. You're a career officer, aren't you?

CAPTAIN KING: Yes, sir.

LITTLEFIELD: Of course you are. COs like me are probably the last thing you need. Crossing over into all sorts of territory.

CAPTAIN KING: Sir?

LITTLEFIELD: Your first name is Lee, is that correct?

CAPTAIN KING: Yes, sir.

LITTLEFIELD: May I call you that this Sunday afternoon?

CAPTAIN KING: Sure.

LITTLEFIELD: Lee, I need your help.

CAPTAIN KING: What do you need, sir?

LITTLEFIELD: I don't know. You see what's happening on base. I can't get in there and make it right. I'm too high up the chain. I can't even have a bull session with an enlisted man. It's not done. I need eyes and ears. You're talking to these boys 'cause of your caseload. What should I know?

CAPTAIN KING: Are you talking to me because I'm black?

LITTLEFIELD: In part.

CAPTAIN KING: Well, I resent that, sir.

LITTLEFIELD: I understand.

CAPTAIN KING: I also joined the corps to escape certain things.

LITTLEFIELD: And did it work out that way?

CAPTAIN KING: Some days.

LITTLEFIELD: What can I do to get the hate out of the barracks?

CAPTAIN KING: Nothing.

LITTLEFIELD: I won't accept that.

CAPTAIN KING: It doesn't start in the barracks. And it doesn't end when you join the corps.

LITTLEFIELD: You feel black marines are treated differently?

CAPTAIN KING: They are treated differently.

LITTLEFIELD: Give me an example.

CAPTAIN KING: I would ask you don't put me in this position, sir.

LITTLEFIELD: Give me an example.

CAPTAIN KING: Housing.

LITTLEFIELD: What are you talking about? On the base?

CAPTAIN KING: No. In Jacksonville. Married black marines looking to rent a place are told there's nothing. And then white marine couples have no problem. The black troops see that, and it causes resentment.

LITTLEFIELD: You know this to be true?

CAPTAIN KING: Yes.

LITTLEFIELD: Give me a name.

CAPTAIN KING: New Beach Apartments.

LITTLEFIELD: New Beach Apartments. I will look into it.

CAPTAIN KING: I'm not asking you to.

LITTLEFIELD: I will look into it.

CAPTAIN KING: All right.

LITTLEFIELD: Did this happen to you?

CAPTAIN KING: No, enlisted men.

LITTLEFIELD: You were an enlisted man.

CAPTAIN KING: That was a long time ago.

LITTLEFIELD: Not that long. Did you encounter prejudice?

CAPTAIN KING: Of course.

LITTLEFIELD (*Outburst*): There's no "of course" about it, dammit!

CAPTAIN KING: Yes, sir.

LITTLEFIELD: But somebody recommended you for Officers Candidate School.

CAPTAIN KING: That's right.

LITTLEFIELD: A white officer?

CAPTAIN KING: Yes, sir.

LITTLEFIELD: Did you experience discrimination in OCS?

CAPTAIN KING: With all due respect, sir, I refuse to indulge myself in a gripe session about my past. If I had a problem, I would've requested MAST. I'm satisfied.

LITTLEFIELD: New Beach Apartments is turning away black marines *now*?

CAPTAIN KING: Yes, sir.

LITTLEFIELD: Why wasn't I told?

CAPTAIN KING: I don't know.

LITTLEFIELD: Why didn't you tell me?

CAPTAIN KING: Frankly, I don't want to be the ombudsman for black marines. I don't want to be treated differently because I'm black. I don't want to be a black officer. I just want to be an officer.

LITTLEFIELD: And that should be possible. I should only have to speak as a commander. But like it or not, there's a man in the uniform. And like it or not, it is one of your accomplishments that you are black and that you hold the rank of captain. Out of the twenty thousand or so officers in the corps, how many black? Three hundred?

CAPTAIN KING: Two hundred and seventy-nine.

LITTLEFIELD: Meg, I imagine you've bitten your tongue a few times during that cup of coffee.

MARGARET: At least six.

LITTLEFIELD: My wife is an SMU girl.

CAPTAIN KING: That's?

MARGARET: Southern Methodist University.

LITTLEFIELD: My point is she's a well-educated white-glove girl. She's fit for more than serving coffee to the likes of us.

CAPTAIN KING: I'm sure.

MARGARET: I don't mind.

LITTLEFIELD: Everybody's got a role to play and none of 'em is a perfect fit. Meg, did you know there was housing discrimination in Jacksonville?

MARGARET: No, but is it surprising?

LITTLEFIELD: I'm surprised.

MARGARET: Well, why?

(Littlefield stands abruptly, offers his hand to King, who stands as well.)

LITTLEFIELD: Captain, I want to thank you for coming over. And for your frankness.

CAPTAIN KING: No problem, sir.

LITTLEFIELD: How many cases in your docket now?

CAPTAIN KING: Six underway, three or four coming in this week.

LITTLEFIELD: Well, we've just got to pull together and get this dull buckle battalion turned around.

CAPTAIN KING: Very good, sir. Mrs. Littlefield, thank you for the coffee and the lemonade.

MARGARET: Your cover, Captain. And take a bun for later.

CAPTAIN KING: Thank you, ma'am.

(King exits. Littlefield pulls off his tie and opens his collar button, starts taking off his shoes.)

LITTLEFIELD *(Muttering)*: Jesus B. Christ!

MARGARET: What is it?

LITTLEFIELD: What was that, you talking about your legs in front of the chaplain?

MARGARET: He'll live. What do you think of him?

LITTLEFIELD: Rub my feet.

MARGARET: Why should I?

LITTLEFIELD: It's Sunday.

MARGARET: Oh, so now it's Sunday. All right. Put 'em up.

(She rubs his feet.)

LITTLEFIELD *(Regarding his feet)*: Oh yeah! *(Moving on)* That chaplain gives me a pain.

MARGARET: You humiliated him.

LITTLEFIELD: Boo-hoo. *(Regarding his foot)* Oh gracious LORD!

MARGARET: Made yourself an enemy.

LITTLEFIELD: So what?

MARGARET: You miss Flanagan.

LITTLEFIELD: Well, the Catholics are just more fun. To them religion's a blood sport.

MARGARET: This one is a bit bland.

LITTLEFIELD: I know the type. He'd like to run the camp. Speaking of which, I heard from Noyes this morning. He's looking to put me up for full bird.

MARGARET: You're not serious!

LITTLEFIELD: What happened to the foot rub?

MARGARET: When were you going to tell me?!

LITTLEFIELD: I *am* telling you.

MARGARET: Morgan!

LITTLEFIELD: Not for a couple of months, but I'm in the promotion zone. Board meets in June. He thinks the ballot will go my way.

MARGARET: Well, isn't that great?

LITTLEFIELD: Yes and no! Before I get kicked upstairs to Regiment, it's my responsibility to make this outfit come out right. Racially.

MARGARET: Morgan.

LITTLEFIELD: Set a standard.

MARGARET: Don't.

LITTLEFIELD: Don't what?

MARGARET: Start pushing people around.

LITTLEFIELD: I'm not pushing, but I have to lead.

MARGARET: You know what your problem is? You're naturally scrappy and you're looking for a good clean fight.

LITTLEFIELD: What's wrong with that?

MARGARET: There aren't any.

LITTLEFIELD: I can tangle with you.

MARGARET: You'd lose. Can't you just admit the corps isn't what it was, and let go.

LITTLEFIELD: The marine corps wasn't ever what it was.

MARGARET: You don't have to tell me.

LITTLEFIELD: But something's come to a head now. There's an opportunity here.

MARGARET: You're not going to be the one to change the world.

LITTLEFIELD: Why not?

MARGARET: Oh God, you just want to be young!

LITTLEFIELD (Stung): What kind of crack is that?

MARGARET: Don't lose your sense of humor now.

LITTLEFIELD: You think I'm old?

MARGARET: You're surrounded by very young men.

LITTLEFIELD: And I can still dominate and lead those men! Is it wrong I want my service to have meant something?

MARGARET: What about my service? When's my turn? I serve you, you serve the corps. When they're done with you, they're done with me.

LITTLEFIELD: I want one shining clean achievement.

MARGARET: Don't you have that?

LITTLEFIELD: No.

MARGARET: I'm ready to get out.

LITTLEFIELD: Don't say that.

MARGARET: What's Joe's picture doing facedown?

LITTLEFIELD: Must've fallen over.

MARGARET: Don't you do that again.

LITTLEFIELD: Don't you talk to me like that.

MARGARET: I'll talk to you.

LITTLEFIELD: Why couldn't the boy have just stayed at Chapel Hill?

MARGARET: Look, I'm with you, but he wants his life to be this big statement like somebody else I know.

LITTLEFIELD: Then let him make a statement, not just cut and run.

MARGARET: He has.

LITTLEFIELD: What?

MARGARET: He has ideals.

LITTLEFIELD: Good! What are they?

MARGARET: You don't want to know.

LITTLEFIELD: Yes, I do.

MARGARET: All right. *(Braces herself)* Love, peace and happiness.

LITTLEFIELD: God in heaven, shoot me where I stand!

MARGARET: He's young!

LITTLEFIELD: He's a man.

MARGARET: So what's yours?

LITTLEFIELD: What?

MARGARET: What's your ideal?

LITTLEFIELD: You.

(They connect.)

MARGARET: Well, you shut me up.

LITTLEFIELD: Full bird and that's it.

MARGARET: Can't you retire?

LITTLEFIELD: Not yet.

MARGARET: I'm here alone now.

LITTLEFIELD: You're not alone. You're with me.

MARGARET: And you're busy. You're afraid to stand still. I halfway think you're afraid of me for Pete's sake! Now that Joe's gone.

LITTLEFIELD: Just stick it out with me, baby. I need you to stick with me for one more go.

MARGARET: What's the point?

LITTLEFIELD: I have to do something. I have to feel like I'm fighting for something worthy and good and on the side of the angels finally.

MARGARET: And you think you can get that?

LITTLEFIELD: Yes I do. I've had a bad taste in my mouth since Korea. You know that. That's been my struggle. Looking for that true opportunity of service.

MARGARET: You want to be a hero.

LITTLEFIELD: Why does a man put on a uniform if he doesn't?

MARGARET: To get girls.

(She takes him in.)

I could shake you.

LITTLEFIELD: Why?

(She shakes her head.)

I'm looking forward to dancing with you at the club. When is that dance?

MARGARET: Three weeks.

LITTLEFIELD: It's because of you. If I wasn't thinking of your good opinion, Meg . . .

MARGARET: Don't lay your military career on me, Skip. I wish you were a folk singer.

LITTLEFIELD: Where should we live when it's over?

MARGARET: Oh, we're going to Colorado.

LITTLEFIELD: Colorado. I'll get a little teaching job.

MARGARET: And we can go hiking in the mountains. I want to climb every one of those mountains with you.

LITTLEFIELD: We will. That's the deal.

MARGARET: Okay. That's the deal. Now. For the love of God, eat this last bun before I do.

(The lights fade.)

SCENE 3

A whistle blows. The battalion gym. Offstage sounds of a basketball bouncing. Captain King is discovered in gym shorts and a regulation T-shirt, sitting on an exercise board doing stomach crunches, counting under his breath. There's also a bench, free weights and a bar for bench presses. A whistle blows. Chaplain White enters, also in gym clothes. He has a sweat up. He sees King and stops, smiling. King doesn't see him for a minute. Then they exchange a look. King's look is blank and inquiring.

CHAPLAIN: Captain King! Captain Lee King! Well, you lit a fire under him!

CAPTAIN KING: Chaplain, how are you?

CHAPLAIN: What'd you talk about that day after I left?

CAPTAIN KING: You're ahead of me.

CHAPLAIN: Colonel Littlefield. These last ten days he's a man on a mission.

CAPTAIN KING: He is?

CHAPLAIN: Have you heard of the Civilian–Military Joint Commission?

CAPTAIN KING: No.

CHAPLAIN: Well, he's convened it.

CAPTAIN KING: You know, my mind was somewhere else. Could you . . .

CHAPLAIN: You turned him around. You want to hear my impression of that day? He was about to come down on the black enlisted men. But after what you had to say, he's attacking on another whole front. He's gone after this apartment complex in Jacksonville? The New River something?

(King gets up and starts adding weights to the bar.)

CAPTAIN KING: The New Beach Apartments?

CHAPLAIN: He's on their tail. He went down there, got proof of discrimination, made the place out of bounds to new military personnel until they get their gear squared away. They've gotta answer to this commission now.

CAPTAIN KING: He proved they were discriminating?

CHAPLAIN: Got back-to-back affidavits. Black couple turned away, white couple approved.

CAPTAIN KING: That was fast.

CHAPLAIN: Like I said. You lit a fire under him. How'd you do it?

CAPTAIN KING: Me?

CHAPLAIN: You set him going.

CAPTAIN KING: The colonel's his own man. I don't know anything about it.

(King lies down to do presses.)

CHAPLAIN: How much weight you got on there?

CAPTAIN KING: A few pounds.

CHAPLAIN: It's enough to crush your gullet. I'll spot you.

(King starts presses.)

I looked for you.

CAPTAIN KING: Excuse me?

CHAPLAIN: At services.

CAPTAIN KING: I don't attend.

CHAPLAIN: You live on base, don't you?

CAPTAIN KING: Yes.

CHAPLAIN: Some of the officers go, you know, just to be role models.

Not married, don't go to services. Where do you get what you need, friend?

(King finishes a round of presses.)

CAPTAIN KING: Look, Chaplain. I'm okay.

CHAPLAIN: You sure?

CAPTAIN KING: Yeah.

CHAPLAIN: You don't want to wait till there's a fire to start a fire department. You want something in place.

CAPTAIN KING: I'm all right.

CHAPLAIN: This is my first time using this gym. A first-rate facility.

CAPTAIN KING: Yeah.

CHAPLAIN: My father used to say, "You take care of the body, the mind will follow." He was a drunkard, but his advice was always sound. Just couldn't take it himself. Sometimes we know what's right, but we haven't the strength to wield the knowledge. You were in the 'Nam, huh?

CAPTAIN KING: Yeah.

CHAPLAIN: One tour?

CAPTAIN KING: Two.

CHAPLAIN: Was it bad?

CAPTAIN KING: It was all right.

CHAPLAIN: I wish I'd been able to go so I could share that with you.

CAPTAIN KING: Thanks.

CHAPLAIN: I got called to the ministry early on, got the deferment. Had a congregation for a bit. But I worried about missing the draft. Didn't want to be a shirker. That's what led me to being a chaplain. I wanted to show my support.

CAPTAIN KING: Good for you.

CHAPLAIN: Funny how things happen. Did a dramatic recitation in high school: "The Face on the Barroom Floor." It's about a man, a painter, destroyed by a woman. He becomes a drunkard. Paints her face on the barroom floor. Then he looks at the beautiful face he has drawn and drops down dead of grief! Right there. Boom. Here I am, a sixteen-year-old boy, reciting this melodramatic poem, tears running down my face without a hair on my chin. Then I just started preaching. Funny how you find your true self. You?

CAPTAIN KING: Me what?

CHAPLAIN: How'd you find your path?

CAPTAIN KING: My mother signed me into the corps.

CHAPLAIN: So you volunteered.

CAPTAIN KING: She volunteered. I was seventeen.

CHAPLAIN: She must be very proud.

CAPTAIN KING: She's dead.

CHAPLAIN: I'm sorry.

CAPTAIN KING: What for? You didn't know her and you don't know me.

CHAPLAIN: You know, Captain, there's something drab and narrow about the way you think.

CAPTAIN KING: Is that right?

CHAPLAIN: Fatalistic. You know a man's whole life can be a prison. He can think he's free. He doesn't see any bars to hold to him, no gate to block his way. But he's trapped utterly and filled with a longing . . . not in his mind. In his heart. He's a prisoner.

(King lies down to start his second round of presses.)

CAPTAIN KING: Well that's okay. Prison isn't so bad.

CHAPLAIN: You've been?

CAPTAIN KING: As a visitor.

CHAPLAIN: To who?

CAPTAIN KING: A family member.

CHAPLAIN: You don't like to show your cards, do you?

CAPTAIN KING: I didn't know we were playing cards.

CHAPLAIN: I think we're playing two games of solitaire and I wonder why we don't just team up?

(King finishes doing his presses and sits up.)

CAPTAIN KING: Listen, Chaplain. How long you been in the corps?

CHAPLAIN: This is my first assignment.

CAPTAIN KING: I'm fine.

(The Chaplain just stands there, staring at him.)

CHAPLAIN: Colonel didn't come to services this week either.

CAPTAIN KING: No?

CHAPLAIN: Kinda cuts the ground out from under me.

CAPTAIN KING: You'll do all right.

CHAPLAIN: I've been reading the minutes of these General Courts you've been adjudicating. Trying to get a sense of what's going on here.

CAPTAIN KING: That's admirable.

CHAPLAIN: I notice you've gone from defending these men to prosecuting them.

(King gets up, starts removing the weights he added to the bar.)

CAPTAIN KING: That's correct.

CHAPLAIN: You're doing the right thing putting these fellows in the brig.

CAPTAIN KING: I'm glad you think so.

CHAPLAIN: Are you comfortable with it?

CAPTAIN KING: No.

CHAPLAIN: If a man does wrong, he needs to be punished.

CAPTAIN KING: Not by me.

CHAPLAIN: What were you raised? Baptist?

CAPTAIN KING: Yes.

CHAPLAIN: Well, where's your sense of sin?

CAPTAIN KING: My other coat I guess.

CHAPLAIN: You think because you've fallen away you've forgotten what's true? *(No answer)* When a man does wrong and you punish him, you're doing him a service.

CAPTAIN KING: Chaplain, I do the work I'm ordered to do. I take the side I'm ordered to take. I'm a tool.

CHAPLAIN: You'd like to think so. But I see through you. You have the reluctant force of morality in you.

CAPTAIN KING: You don't know me.

CHAPLAIN: Let me ask you something. Why do you take the weights off the bar after you're done?

CAPTAIN KING: To leave things the way I found them.

CHAPLAIN: As if you'd never been here. As if you never existed. You'd like to leave not a footprint in the sand. That's not why God put you on this earth.

CAPTAIN KING: Look. I'm gonna hit the shower.

CHAPLAIN: I will find my use in Sixth Marines.

CAPTAIN KING: I have no doubt.

CHAPLAIN: I'm not here just to pretty up the place. So if you need advice about anything. If you want to speak to someone outside the chain of command . . .

CAPTAIN KING: I'm fine.

CHAPLAIN: What's said to me in confidence is privileged.

CAPTAIN KING: I'm fine, I said.

CHAPLAIN: Consider coming to services.

CAPTAIN KING: Have a nice day.

CHAPLAIN: Life *is* melodramatic, Captain. That's been my experience. Like it or not. Good and evil in a struggle to prevail. And guess what? Good wins every time.

CAPTAIN KING: I'll wait for the movie. *(Goes)*
CHAPLAIN: "I'll wait for the movie"? *(Laughs)* That's good.

(He sees himself in a mirror. Recites:)

> Say, boys, if you give me just another whiskey I'll
> be glad, and I'll draw right here a picture of the
> face that drove me mad. Give me that piece of
> chalk with which you mark the baseball score—
> you shall see the lovely Madeline upon the bar-
> room floor.

(The lights fade.)

SCENE 4

The Paradise Point Officers Club. Margaret, in evening wear, sits alone on a dais at a table for six. There are many used glasses, and a little floral centerpiece. The dinner dishes have been removed. She's bored. She's listening to a bad band sing a song like "One Is the Loneliest Number" in the distance. She nods and weakly waves at unseen guests. The song finishes. Distant applause. Colonel Littlefield arrives. He's in a formal military dinner jacket. He's limping a bit. He's had a couple of drinks, but he's fine.

LITTLEFIELD: How you doing, Meg?
MARGARET: Bored.
LITTLEFIELD: You usually like these things.
MARGARET: We usually dance.
LITTLEFIELD: Well, I stepped on a nail.
MARGARET: A week ago.
LITTLEFIELD: It hit the bone.
MARGARET: You're walking.

LITTLEFIELD: Not in a forgiving frame of mind, huh?

MARGARET: What's with you?

LITTLEFIELD: I am the host of this dinner. I have to talk to everybody or half of everybody at least. So I have to walk around. But I can tell you, I'd rather be sitting down.

MARGARET: Hmm.

LITTLEFIELD: What's the matter?

MARGARET: I'm at a table for six alone.

LITTLEFIELD: Well, get up and circulate.

MARGARET: So you're not sitting down?

LITTLEFIELD: General Noyes just came in. I have a few things we have to talk about.

MARGARET: Fine. Go talk to General Noyes. *(He's almost gone)* And take your time.

(He struggles a second, then goes. After a moment, Margaret pulls a flower from the floral arrangement and sticks it behind her ear. She pulls out a paperback book and begins to read. Captain King walks by with two drinks.)

CAPTAIN KING: Good evening, ma'am.

MARGARET: Who's the other drink for?

CAPTAIN KING: Me.

MARGARET: In that case, take a seat a minute, Captain. I am marooned here.

CAPTAIN KING *(Sitting)*: I'd be delighted. What are you reading?

MARGARET: *On Aggression*, Konrad Lorenz. Have you read it?

CAPTAIN KING: No.

MARGARET: I'm putting it away.

CAPTAIN KING *(Starts to rise)*: No, go on with your reading, I'm interrupting.

MARGARET: Hardly. I was just trying to appear to have an activity. Please.

CAPTAIN KING: *On Aggression*. Who's he talking about?

MARGARET: Animals, humans, humans, animals. Why we kill each other.

CAPTAIN KING: Why?

MARGARET: My opinion? He doesn't know. I'm going to change the subject. Don't you love the name of this place? The Paradise Point Officers Club. Sounds like what?

CAPTAIN KING: *Tender Is the Night.*

MARGARET: So you do read!

CAPTAIN KING: Yes.

MARGARET: I didn't mean that to be pejorative.

CAPTAIN KING: It's okay. Actually, I don't read many novels.

MARGARET: Neither do I. I like idea books. Books that put forward a theory.

CAPTAIN KING: Why?

MARGARET: Because men love their theories, and do things to the world to prove their ideas are correct. So I figure if I read enough of these books, I'll understand men.

CAPTAIN KING: Why would you want to?

MARGARET: There's so many of them around.

CAPTAIN KING: I think you're going to have to read a lot.

MARGARET: Don't flatter yourself. Most men are just emotion.

CAPTAIN KING: I thought that was women.

MARGARET: When women get upset, they cry. When men get upset, they see an international threat.

CAPTAIN KING: You're pretty sharp.

MARGARET: You can follow the game better from the bench. What do you read?

CAPTAIN KING: History mostly.

MARGARET: I need something more up-to-date. What do you get from history?

CAPTAIN KING: I don't know. That progress doesn't need me. It'll happen anyway. The past runs out of steam and things change. History doesn't need anybody. I like that.

MARGARET: What if something comes up and you are needed?

CAPTAIN KING: Well, I guess I wouldn't like that. The colonel's limping a little.

MARGARET: He stepped on a nail. It's your fault. He went down to those apartments you told him about . . .

CAPTAIN KING: New Beach.

MARGARET: Disguised as a civilian. Or at least a man of no particular rank. And in the course of sleuthing out racial wrongdoing, he stepped on a nail. Came home with one sock and a limp.

CAPTAIN KING: You have to give it to him. He got something done.

MARGARET: Why is that so important again?

CAPTAIN KING: Some men need to do deeds.

MARGARET: You?

CAPTAIN KING: No. Would you like one of these before the ice melts? Rum and Coke.

MARGARET: Sure. Thanks.

CAPTAIN KING: Got a taste for them in Cuba.

MARGARET: You were stationed at Guantánamo?

CAPTAIN KING: For a year.

MARGARET: Was it boring?

CAPTAIN KING: I never thought about that.

MARGARET: Why not?

CAPTAIN KING: No, it wasn't boring.

MARGARET: What did you do?

CAPTAIN KING: Paperwork.

MARGARET: And it wasn't boring?

CAPTAIN KING: No.

MARGARET: Do you think that there's some monumental life out there that you should be living?

CAPTAIN KING: No.

MARGARET: Me neither. But what if we're wrong, Captain?

CAPTAIN KING: I don't think big ideas are that important.

MARGARET: Then what keeps you going?

CAPTAIN KING: I don't know.

MARGARET: Love?

CAPTAIN KING: Certainly not. I don't believe in invisible things.

MARGARET: I'm invisible.

CAPTAIN KING: So why do you think we kill each other?

MARGARET: Lust.

CAPTAIN KING: I think I'm gonna . . . stretch my legs. If you'll excuse me, ma'am?

MARGARET: Of course.

(King gets up as Littlefield arrives with a bottle of champagne.)

LITTLEFIELD: Where you going, Captain? Sit down a minute. Has Meg been entertaining?

MARGARET: I don't think so.

LITTLEFIELD: Well, let me see if I can give you a goose. I just talked to General Noyes and he has approved my appointment of you as my XO.

(Littlefield pours glasses of champagne.)

CAPTAIN KING: What?

LITTLEFIELD: Effective damn near immediately.

CAPTAIN KING: Sir, I'm . . .

LITTLEFIELD: Hence the champagne. Executive Officer, second in command of First Battalion, Sixth Marines.

MARGARET: Well, Captain, congratulations!

CAPTAIN KING: You can't be serious, sir. I can't believe it.

LITTLEFIELD: Don't blame you. You just jumped over three other captains. There's a promotion percolating there, too. You're in line to make Major—pretty outrageously young Major—history, too, maybe.

MARGARET: Good for you!

LITTLEFIELD: Wasn't dead certain until I had one more conversation with Noyes, but I've had it now. You're in.

CAPTAIN KING: Why?

LITTLEFIELD: Because you are the right man for the post. You have done exemplary work as a judge advocate. You have meritoriously commanded troops in combat. Your record as an officer is outstanding in every way.

CAPTAIN KING: More than the other three captains?

LITTLEFIELD: There are many factors at play in my decision.

CAPTAIN KING: What did you mean I'm in a position to make history?

LITTLEFIELD: You have a shot now down the road given this of commanding a battalion.

CAPTAIN KING: And no black man's ever commanded a marine battalion.

LITTLEFIELD: That is correct.

CAPTAIN KING: So I was chosen over these other men because of my color.

LITTLEFIELD: You were chosen because I chose you. You.

MARGARET: I'm going to go powder my nose. Congratulations, Captain.

(The men rise with her. She goes.)

CAPTAIN KING: I'm uncomfortable, sir.

LITTLEFIELD: Why?

CAPTAIN KING: It's obvious.

LITTLEFIELD: We have a morale problem among our black marines. I am taking the steps necessary to address that situation. I believe this will help.

CAPTAIN KING: I don't want to be used.

LITTLEFIELD: Well, you will be used in whatever goddamn way best benefits the corps. I don't get to live a life of self-interest. Nor do you. That's what service is about.

CAPTAIN KING: I don't want the attention.

LITTLEFIELD: Captain . . .

CAPTAIN KING: I just want to disappear into my uniform. That's all I've ever wanted. I don't want to have my identity asserted in an individual way. It's unmilitary, sir. It's unmilitary. And I am very much of a military disposition.

LITTLEFIELD: Listen, Lee, in the armed services, you either go forward or fall out. You make rank or make for the door. Which is it gonna be?

CAPTAIN KING: Of course I'll accept the post if you insist.

LITTLEFIELD: I do. Good man. You'll do this thing, accept the post. 'Cause you're not just yourself. You're many men. You represent change. Same as combat. Point man takes the heat. This time it's you.

CAPTAIN KING: Very good, sir. I think I'll say good night.

LITTLEFIELD: Good man.

(They shake hands and King goes. Littlefield lights a cigarette. Margaret returns.)

MARGARET: Smoking?

LITTLEFIELD: One.

MARGARET: You look so dissatisfied.

LITTLEFIELD: I'm just determined.

MARGARET: Do you have a new XO?

LITTLEFIELD: Oh yes.

MARGARET: It's funny.

LITTLEFIELD: What?

MARGARET: You want to make your mark. And that black captain, he just wants to slip away.

LITTLEFIELD: What do you want?

MARGARET: You.

LITTLEFIELD: Now what kind of thing is that to say?

MARGARET: Who you doing this for exactly? The captain? He wishes you'd lay off. Who's the show for? Joe?

LITTLEFIELD: No.

MARGARET: Show your son you're part of the noble new thing?

LITTLEFIELD: I don't have to do a damn thing more than be who I've been for twenty years to set my son an example. And what good did it do? He's a draft dodger.

MARGARET: Yeah, he is.

LITTLEFIELD: What the hell is that?

MARGARET: I don't know.

LITTLEFIELD: My son.

MARGARET: Our son.

LITTLEFIELD: Ran out on the goddamn draft.

MARGARET: It took courage.

LITTLEFIELD: Courage? Holding a position against hostile fire takes courage. Going to Toronto takes an afternoon in a car.

MARGARET: He doesn't believe in the war.

LITTLEFIELD: He has a duty to report for service.

MARGARET: When did he agree to that?

LITTLEFIELD: The day he was born on American soil!

MARGARET: I was there the day he was born. He didn't say anything. (Pause) Look, he doesn't get it.

LITTLEFIELD: What?

MARGARET: He thinks this war is crazy.

LITTLEFIELD: Do you think I understood what the hell I was doing in Korea? Nobody did. But I went.

MARGARET: That's not much of an argument.

LITTLEFIELD: Well, I'm not a philosopher.

MARGARET: Maybe you should be a little bit.

LITTLEFIELD: Whose side are you on?

MARGARET: A man should know why he fights.

LITTLEFIELD: Him doing this, it's against me.

MARGARET: Maybe.

LITTLEFIELD: Canada.

MARGARET: I'll get his address. You'll write him a letter.

LITTLEFIELD: Is that an order?

MARGARET: A good letter.

LITTLEFIELD: All right.

MARGARET: Good man.

LITTLEFIELD: I wish I was better.

MARGARET: You're good enough.

LITTLEFIELD: No.

(Music. A slow song starts to play, perhaps The Dave Clark Five's "Because.")

Maybe I have been drifting a bit.

MARGARET: I miss it when I can't find the diamond in your eye.

LITTLEFIELD: I'm here. Okay, I'm here now.

MARGARET: All right.

LITTLEFIELD: Come on. Let's dance one and go home.

(She comes to him. They dance. They stop. They kiss. The lights fade.)

SCENE 5

Battalion headquarters. The Executive Officer's office. Captain King is looking at a file. He's in khakis. His phone rings.

CAPTAIN KING: Yes, Sergeant? Send him in.

(Private First Class Evan Davis knocks on the open door three times.)

Enter.

(PFC Davis enters and comes to attention. He's in utilities. He is from Beaufort, South Carolina. He's a poor white Southern man, twenty years old. He's had a rough life. He is quietly distraught.)

PRIVATE DAVIS: PFC Evan Davis reporting, sir.

CAPTAIN KING: State your business, Marine.

PRIVATE DAVIS: I request transfer to WESTPAC, FMF, Ground Forces.

CAPTAIN KING: Vietnam.

PRIVATE DAVIS: Yes, sir.

CAPTAIN KING: The chaplain sent you over, huh?

PRIVATE DAVIS: Yes, sir.

CAPTAIN KING: Well, first of all, we're out of Vietnam basically, Private.

PRIVATE DAVIS: I know of a man at Cherry Point got orders last week.

CAPTAIN KING: Cherry Point's the Air Wing. They still need some tech types in Da Nang, but you're in the infantry, Private. Nobody from Infantry's going now.

PRIVATE DAVIS: I'm requesting I go.

CAPTAIN KING: Even if there was a billet, I have no reason to single you out for special consideration, Davis. You had an unauthorized absence three days last week.

PRIVATE DAVIS: I had a problem.

CAPTAIN KING: You still do. That's on your record now. How could I push for your reassignment? There's no justification. You are not recommendable.

PRIVATE DAVIS: The chaplain said I should talk to you.

CAPTAIN KING: That's another thing. You jumped the chain of command. You should have gone to your company commander.

PRIVATE DAVIS: The chaplain said I should talk to you.

CAPTAIN KING: Well, he was in error. You should have gone first to your company commander.

PRIVATE DAVIS: The chaplain said you.

CAPTAIN KING: Well, we've talked. And there's nothing going to come of it. Request denied. Return to your company.

PRIVATE DAVIS: The chaplain said if you refused me, I could request MAST to the colonel.

(King becomes cautious. Where is this going?)

CAPTAIN KING: That's your right. Every marine has the right to request MAST up the chain of command. But I can tell you your transfer will be denied and the colonel will not take it well that you wasted his time. Are you requesting MAST to the colonel?

PRIVATE DAVIS: I'd rather work it out with you, sir.

CAPTAIN KING: But we're done. It's a dead end.

PRIVATE DAVIS: I've got to get that transfer.

CAPTAIN KING: Why?

PRIVATE DAVIS: I'd rather not say.

CAPTAIN KING: Well, I don't know what to tell you, Private. You're not giving me much to work with.

PRIVATE DAVIS: Please help me.

CAPTAIN KING: I don't see how I can.

PRIVATE DAVIS: All right then. All right. I would like to request MAST to the colonel, sir.

CAPTAIN KING: He's not going to like it.

PRIVATE DAVIS: No, sir.

CAPTAIN KING: It says here you're married.

PRIVATE DAVIS: Yes, sir.

CAPTAIN KING: You a brown bagger? She with you?

PRIVATE DAVIS: In Jacksonville. Yes, sir.

CAPTAIN KING: Why don't you talk this over with her.

PRIVATE DAVIS: We have had that conversation. Sir, I am requesting MAST to see the colonel.

CAPTAIN KING: All right. I advise against it. But I'll fill out the forms and send on your file. You'll be notified of your appointment.

PRIVATE DAVIS: Thank you, sir.

CAPTAIN KING: Dismissed.

(Private Davis starts to go, then stops.)

I said dismissed. What is it?

(No answer.)

What is it?

(Private Davis starts to shake. King gets up.)

What's the matter?

PRIVATE DAVIS: He laid my wife.

CAPTAIN KING: What? Who?

PRIVATE DAVIS: The colonel. He laid my wife.

(King rushes over and shuts the door.)

CAPTAIN KING: What are you talking about?

PRIVATE DAVIS: I've gotta get outta here!

CAPTAIN KING: Take it easy! Sit down.

PRIVATE DAVIS: I don't wanna sit down! I can't sit down! I gotta get off this base! Don't make me talk to him! Just get me orders. Send me to 'Nam! I've gotta get away!

CAPTAIN KING: How do you know this? I mean . . . It can't be true.

PRIVATE DAVIS: He was in civvies. He stepped on a nail. Karen brought him up, made him take off his shoe. She soaked his foot.

CAPTAIN KING: Where's your housing?

PRIVATE DAVIS: New Beach Apartments.

(This floors King.)

CAPTAIN KING: New Beach . . . Did you tell the chaplain this?
PRIVATE DAVIS: Yes, sir. In confidence.
CAPTAIN KING: What did he say?
PRIVATE DAVIS: To tell you.
CAPTAIN KING: Why me?!
PRIVATE DAVIS: I don't want to see the colonel, sir. I just want to go fight.
CAPTAIN KING: Maybe I can get you transferred to another stateside base.
PRIVATE DAVIS: That won't do it. I want to go to Vietnam.
CAPTAIN KING: I can't do that! There's no way I can get that through!
PRIVATE DAVIS: Could the colonel?
CAPTAIN KING: I don't know!
PRIVATE DAVIS: I have to go to him then.
CAPTAIN KING: Don't! Let me think about this. Give me a day. I'll send word to you.
PRIVATE DAVIS: I can't stick it here long, sir. I'm in hell. She was everything to me. Now I can't look at her. I just want to go.
CAPTAIN KING: I'll do something.
PRIVATE DAVIS: Thank you, Captain. I don't want to see him, you know? She was my little girl. And now she's . . . It'll never be the same. So I don't want to see him. But I will if I have to.
CAPTAIN KING: Why do you want to go to Vietnam?
PRIVATE DAVIS: To die.
CAPTAIN KING: Go back to your unit.
PRIVATE DAVIS: That's why I was gone the three days, sir. 'Cause a this. So I'd appreciate if you didn't hold that against me.

CAPTAIN KING: Go, go. Let me think on this.

(Private Davis goes. King is in shock. He picks up the phone to make a call. Decides against it. Hangs up. Picks up the receiver again. Hangs up again. Picks up the base directory, looks up a number. Picks up the phone a third time and dials:)

Hello, Chaplain? It's Captain King. Yeah, he just left. Yeah, he did. Well, I'm stunned. I don't know. No, it's not illegal per se. Well, it's Conduct Unbecoming. And it would end a career like a rifle shot . . . Exactly.

(A knock at the door.)

Who is it?

(The door opens. It's Colonel Littlefield, smiling. He whispers:)

LITTLEFIELD: Thought I'd see how you're doing.
CAPTAIN KING *(Into phone)*: Let me call you back. *(Hangs up, starts to stand)* Good afternoon, Colonel. I can come into your office if you'd like.
LITTLEFIELD: Don't bother with that. We're colleagues now. You settling in all right?
CAPTAIN KING: Fine.
LITTLEFIELD: I thought it might be good if we came up with a map for the next month or so. What's the matter?
CAPTAIN KING: I just had some . . . I just had a piece of upsetting news.
LITTLEFIELD: Anything I can help with?
CAPTAIN KING: No, sir.
LITTLEFIELD: Personal?
CAPTAIN KING: Yes.

LITTLEFIELD: You need some leave?

CAPTAIN KING: No, there's a . . . It's not a matter of that.

LITTLEFIELD: Good. I can't spare you right now.

CAPTAIN KING: I just need an hour or two.

LITTLEFIELD: Well, take it. Walk over to the PX. Buy yourself something. We can talk later.

CAPTAIN KING: Thank you, sir.

LITTLEFIELD: You hear about the New Beach Apartments? We straightened that out.

CAPTAIN KING: I did hear. I didn't think you'd be able to do anything about it. Since it's civilian.

LITTLEFIELD: That's true. But all their business is with the military.

CAPTAIN KING: Well. You did it.

LITTLEFIELD: Not a bad place to live.

CAPTAIN KING: You went into an apartment?

LITTLEFIELD: Yes. Well, I'll let you go.

CAPTAIN KING: May I drop in and speak to you later?

LITTLEFIELD: Of course.

CAPTAIN KING: Sixteen hundred okay?

LITTLEFIELD: No, actually that's no good. I've got to go up to Regiment. You know what? Come by my place for dinner. I'll leave a time for you after I talk to Meg.

CAPTAIN KING: Yes, sir. Fine.

LITTLEFIELD: You like meatloaf?

CAPTAIN KING: Sure.

LITTLEFIELD: Good. See you then. Go have a cup of coffee or something.

(Littlefield goes, closing the door behind him. After a moment, King starts to dial again. The lights fade.)

SCENE 6

The lights come up on a park bench on which sits Chaplain White. He's in marine corps khakis. He's unpacking a lunch from a brown paper bag: a sandwich in wax paper, a napkin, a thermos of iced tea. He pours a cup. Captain King approaches.

CHAPLAIN: Mind if I don't get up, Captain? I've just got my lunch laid out.

CAPTAIN KING: No, no.

CHAPLAIN: Peanut butter, golden raisins and honey on pumpernickel bread. Every day.

CAPTAIN KING: Sounds good.

CHAPLAIN: My wife's tired of making it, says it's a sticky mess.

CAPTAIN KING: Yeah. Sticky.

CHAPLAIN: But. I've got two napkins.

CAPTAIN KING: Thanks for coming.

CHAPLAIN: Would you mind? You talk a little. Let me just eat this.

(King is at a loss.)

CAPTAIN KING: Well, you know.

CHAPLAIN: No, sir. I do not know. Sure I talked to Private Davis. But then he talked to you. And did you talk to the colonel?

CAPTAIN KING: Not about this.

CHAPLAIN: Are you going to try to send the boy to Vietnam?

CAPTAIN KING: It's not in my power.

CHAPLAIN: Could Colonel Littlefield?

CAPTAIN KING: It's a stretch. I don't know.

CHAPLAIN: If the colonel could do it, and wanted to do it, did do it, what then? Would that be all right with you?

CAPTAIN KING: I don't know.

CHAPLAIN: Keep talking.

CAPTAIN KING: I'm having trouble just understanding this. That a man of such high rank would put everything on the line . . .

CHAPLAIN: Of course it's shocking.

CAPTAIN KING: Doesn't make sense.

CHAPLAIN: Logic alone can't stay the wrongful act. Sin doesn't make sense most of the time, but we sin anyway.

CAPTAIN KING: He's a marine corps colonel.

CHAPLAIN: Emperors, popes and presidents have gambled their reputations on a dalliance. What's a marine corps colonel? He's a man. Human nature.

CAPTAIN KING: But why would he do it?

CHAPLAIN: That's not the question. Why wouldn't he do it? That's the question. Given that he believes in nothing, there was nothing keeping him from falling down but habit. And habit is not enough, friend, when the flesh reaches out for what it wants.

CAPTAIN KING: Still.

CHAPLAIN: Did you see the anguish on that young man's face?

CAPTAIN KING: I did.

CHAPLAIN: Did you believe that?

CAPTAIN KING: I don't know. Maybe not.

(No answer. The Chaplain eats and stares and waits.)

Yes, I believed it.

CHAPLAIN: Why?

CAPTAIN KING: Why would a man come in with a story like that? I know if I chase it down, it will turn out to be true. The man knew Colonel Littlefield had stepped on a nail. Such a shit-ass, trivial, damning little piece of evidence.

CHAPLAIN: Did the private tell you he has the colonel's sock?

CAPTAIN KING: No.

CHAPLAIN: Well, he does. So I repeat to you. If Colonel Little-field can succeed in getting PFC Davis orders for Vietnam, would that be all right with you?

CAPTAIN KING: Why did you bypass his company commander? Why did you send that man to me?

CHAPLAIN: I don't know the company commander.

CAPTAIN KING: You hardly know me.

CHAPLAIN: I know you're uneasy in your skin, and I'm not talking about color now.

CAPTAIN KING: What are you talking about?

CHAPLAIN: Conscience! Right and wrong! Things you don't do and things you have to do.

CAPTAIN KING: You mean to see him ruined over this. Don't you?

CHAPLAIN: Do you know the story of David and Bathsheba?

CAPTAIN KING: Am I right?

CHAPLAIN: Do you know the story of David and Bathsheba?

CAPTAIN KING: Yes, I know it!

CHAPLAIN: I don't think you do. Not really. David was a great king overseeing a war from his capital. He was fifty years of age. How old is the colonel?

CAPTAIN KING: I don't know.

CHAPLAIN: One night he spied a voluptuous woman bathing on her roof. He sent for her. She was the wife of a common soldier named Uriah.

CAPTAIN KING: I know the story. David slept with her and, to get rid of the husband, sent him into battle. And the man was killed.

CHAPLAIN: Story doesn't end there. The woman had David's son. But God was mad! David wasn't just a man, he was a king! And kings must bear the burden as well as the crown! So God killed the baby. Blood for blood. And the man suffered incredibly. God was satisfied, and in the fullness of time, David had another son and named him Solomon. And Solomon *was* wisdom. Do you understand, Captain?

CAPTAIN KING: No.

CHAPLAIN: He's got to pay the price, then good may come of it.

CAPTAIN KING: You say.

CHAPLAIN: I do say.

CAPTAIN KING: There's an unwritten code. I'm his XO. I'm supposed to protect him.

CHAPLAIN: I don't think you can.

CAPTAIN KING: If I go to the general, it's the end of my career, too.

CHAPLAIN: I doubt that.

CAPTAIN KING: Then you don't know the military. *(Pause)* I hate you bastards, every goddamn one of you!

CHAPLAIN: What are you talking about?

CAPTAIN KING: Power.

CHAPLAIN: It's not me you hate. It's responsibility. That's what you despise, Captain. You're turned around. You despise your own goodness. You wish you didn't contain it.

CAPTAIN KING: I didn't do anything! Why should anything fall to me?!

CHAPLAIN: Who hasn't felt that?

CAPTAIN KING: The man came to you!

CHAPLAIN: And then you.

CAPTAIN KING: You sent him to me!

CHAPLAIN: Yes, I did.

CAPTAIN KING: So I'll send him on to the colonel and he can do as he sees fit.

CHAPLAIN: What if he sees fit to do wrong?

CAPTAIN KING: Then you can squawk.

CHAPLAIN: The man told me in confidence. He asked me not to speak and I'm bound by that. But you're not.

CAPTAIN KING: It's up to the colonel.

CHAPLAIN: Is it? Wouldn't it be irresponsible and in fact a violation of the spirit, if not the letter of the Uniform Code of Military Justice, for you to allow that victimized young man to have to *petition* the very fellow who defiled his young wife?!

CAPTAIN KING: Why are you doing this?

CHAPLAIN: Doesn't matter.

CAPTAIN KING: You're out to get him!

CHAPLAIN: It doesn't matter.

CAPTAIN KING: He's doing a lot of good things.

CHAPLAIN: For the blacks on the base.

CAPTAIN KING: What does that mean? You don't approve?

CHAPLAIN: I didn't say that.

CAPTAIN KING: Well, goddammit, Chaplain, what do you say?

CHAPLAIN: That there's a higher law than the UCMJ! That there's a higher law than the understanding among officers or your personal sense of what is just! And you know it! Captain! You know it. So even though my hands are tied by a promise I made to an abused young man, I have nothing to worry about because *you* will do the right thing. Even if it disgusts you. And even if you suspect my reasons.

CAPTAIN KING: How do you know that?

CHAPLAIN: Because of your relationship with God.

CAPTAIN KING: I don't believe in God.

CHAPLAIN: I don't believe in God either. He's a fact! He is a force in your heart just as he is in mine. You can leave him out of your calculations if you want. Doesn't matter. You'll still feel his opinion as the right and its opposite as the wrong! All you hairy-chested men of authority make me laugh. Where do you think authority comes from? Do you think it's arbitrary? Colonel Littlefield has no authority in himself. The President of the United States has no authority in himself. We derive what strength we have from a power outside of ourselves.

CAPTAIN KING: The president gets his power from the people.

CHAPLAIN: And where do the people get it? That snake eats its own tail. Only a man who acknowledges the divine has the humility to command.

CAPTAIN KING: You nominating yourself?

CHAPLAIN: No, sir.

CAPTAIN KING: The military gets its power from a democratically elected commander-in-chief!

CHAPLAIN: Wake up. The concept of obedience is a house of cards if you believe in nothing. A man who obeys only to avoid confrontation is made of repeated opinions and smoke. Why do you think the colonel's son ran out on his military obligation?

CAPTAIN KING: What's that got to do with anything?

CHAPLAIN: Because his father the colonel doesn't know why he gets up in the morning, that's why! Because his father the colonel has no way to tell right from wrong, no less why he should be obeyed and followed.

CAPTAIN KING: What do you want?

CHAPLAIN: I'm glad we're having this conversation.

CAPTAIN KING: What do you want?

CHAPLAIN: Doesn't matter what I want. Doesn't matter what you want either. Only thing that matters is what you do. You're going to have to deal with that young man. He's waiting and he won't keep waiting.

CAPTAIN KING: I'm not afraid of you.

CHAPLAIN: Yes, you are.

CAPTAIN KING: The day will come.

CHAPLAIN: Oh, we have an appointment, sir, I know that, and I will be waiting! But your point of view is still under construction and I must be patient. It's pride, you know.

CAPTAIN KING: What?

CHAPLAIN: That keeps you from accepting somebody else's truth. Another man. Another culture. Another race. I would die for what I believe. Can you say as much?

CAPTAIN KING: I can do better. I'd die for nothing at all.

CHAPLAIN: Pride.

CAPTAIN KING: Maybe the colonel didn't do it.

CHAPLAIN: Captain, there's what you want to believe, and then there's the truth.

CAPTAIN KING: I'm going to ask him.

CHAPLAIN: Go ahead. But if he lies, you be a man.

CAPTAIN KING: He's my superior officer.

CHAPLAIN: But his authority rests on right actions. If he's corrupt, he's done!

CAPTAIN KING: You wanted to know what it was like in Vietnam? It was like this. A knot in my stomach! Because nothing was right! And nothing's been right since!

CHAPLAIN: It's been going on longer than that.

CAPTAIN KING: What?

CHAPLAIN: You've been feeling wrong since you were born, haven't you?

(Pause. A standoff.)

Can't face the demands of your own character. My father was the same way. That's why he drank.

CAPTAIN KING: What are you talking about?

CHAPLAIN: You're a leader, but you run from it. When a man runs from his own character, the world gets smaller and smaller. Like the pig chute at the slaughterhouse. I'm sorry you suffer.

CAPTAIN KING: Drop dead.

CHAPLAIN: I know you'll make the right choice. I believe you always have.

CAPTAIN KING: What are you? You're not a man at all. You're a cold stone bastard.

CHAPLAIN: Morality is not a human thing. It's like the ocean. It moves with us and against us.

(King watches the Chaplain wipe his hands with a napkin.)

You ought to drop by services next Sunday.

CAPTAIN KING: You can wipe those hands all afternoon. You'll never be done.

(King walks off. The Chaplain calls after him:)

CHAPLAIN: Oh, I'll be all right. I have two napkins.

(The Chaplain gets up and walks off. The lights fade.)

SCENE 7

The Littlefield home. Colonel Littlefield is in civilian clothes, an Izod shirt, khaki trousers, spit-shined shoes. He's reading a report. The door-bell rings. He gets up to answer it. Margaret comes out of the kitchen. She's wearing an apron, she's a little harried.

LITTLEFIELD: I'll get it.

MARGARET: I couldn't get Sandy's wife off the phone so you just have to give me fifteen minutes. I've got to get some beer.

LITTLEFIELD: I don't need a beer.

MARGARET: I do!

(She disappears into the foyer, opens the front door, and greets Captain King:)

(Offstage) Hey, Captain.

CAPTAIN KING (*Offstage*): Good evening, ma'am.

MARGARET (*Offstage*): You should've come in civvies.

CAPTAIN KING (*Offstage*): Didn't have time to change.

MARGARET (*Offstage*): Get him a drink, Morgan! I'll be back in fifteen minutes.

(*The door slams. Margaret is gone. King comes in. Littlefield shakes his hand.*)

LITTLEFIELD: Captain, what are you drinking?

CAPTAIN KING: I would have a drink.

LITTLEFIELD: You like that rum and Coke, right?

CAPTAIN KING: If you have it, sir.

LITTLEFIELD: We can dispense with the "sir" tonight. We'll talk shop, but this is social.

CAPTAIN KING: Your wife.

LITTLEFIELD: What about her?

CAPTAIN KING: She'll be back in fifteen minutes?

LITTLEFIELD: About.

(*Sets about making King a drink.*)

CAPTAIN KING: Okay.

LITTLEFIELD: You all right? That personal matter still weighing on you?

CAPTAIN KING: Yes, I guess so.

LITTLEFIELD: I was just reading a Defense Department report about race and the military. Very interesting. They think we're past the worst. They think things are going to get better from here. Maybe so.

CAPTAIN KING: We don't have much time, sir. I don't think I should be here when your wife comes back.

LITTLEFIELD (*Stops making the drink*): What? What are you talking about?

CAPTAIN KING: I'm in turmoil, sir. I don't want to go into something, and I don't see any way around it.

LITTLEFIELD: What?

CAPTAIN KING: I don't want to be here.

LITTLEFIELD: Well, you're here.

CAPTAIN KING: I don't want this job.

LITTLEFIELD: What job?

CAPTAIN KING: Being me, I guess.

LITTLEFIELD: Spit it out.

CAPTAIN KING: Did you sleep with an enlisted man's wife?

(An awful pause.)

LITTLEFIELD: Yes.

CAPTAIN KING: Jesus Christ.

LITTLEFIELD: Her husband found out?

CAPTAIN KING: Yes, sir. He's a PFC. He went to the chaplain with it and the chaplain sent him to me.

LITTLEFIELD: Straight to you?

CAPTAIN KING: Yes, sir.

LITTLEFIELD: And what are you going to do?

CAPTAIN KING: I don't want to do anything. The man's asked for orders. He's distraught. He wants to be sent to Vietnam.

LITTLEFIELD: Vietnam?

CAPTAIN KING: Yes, sir.

LITTLEFIELD: Does he have a clean record?

CAPTAIN KING: No.

LITTLEFIELD: What's on there?

CAPTAIN KING: He went UA for three days. Over this.

LITTLEFIELD: That's not too bad. We could remove that. It wouldn't be—

CAPTAIN KING *(Shocked)*: You're not allowed to remove anything from a man's record!

(Pause.)

LITTLEFIELD: No, of course not.

CAPTAIN KING: If he doesn't get the orders he wants, I think it's all going to come out.

LITTLEFIELD: Well, he's not going to get those orders, so it is all going to come out.

CAPTAIN KING: Yes, sir.

LITTLEFIELD: I just went down there to do something good. And I stepped on a nail. I don't know where the hell my driver went! . . . And this girl, you know, one of those small-town girls who marry servicemen, she insisted on taking me in so she could soak my foot. She looked up at me with this . . . she looked up at me, and I responded. *(Starts to break down, then recovers)* And because of that . . . I mean what am I supposed to do?

CAPTAIN KING: Why'd you do it?

LITTLEFIELD: I don't know.

CAPTAIN KING: You had to realize—

LITTLEFIELD: I didn't realize anything. It wasn't about thinking.

CAPTAIN KING: It's going to come out.

LITTLEFIELD: When?

CAPTAIN KING: Tomorrow. He's requested MAST to ask you to get him those orders.

LITTLEFIELD: So send him to me.

CAPTAIN KING: I can't.

LITTLEFIELD: Maybe I can talk him out of it.

CAPTAIN KING: Sir?

LITTLEFIELD: Get him transferred to Cherry Point, the Air Wing. The base commander and I go back. He might be able to get him a critical MOS. The boy could be stationed in Da Nang. It'd be Vietnam, but he wouldn't be in harm's way . . .

CAPTAIN KING: I can't send him to you!

LITTLEFIELD: Why not?

CAPTAIN KING: You know why! Because it's wrong, sir! It's wrong! You slept with the boy's wife! And he's under your command!

LITTLEFIELD: Just send him to me.

CAPTAIN KING: No, sir!

LITTLEFIELD: And if I give you a direct order?

CAPTAIN KING: Don't!

LITTLEFIELD: But if I do?

CAPTAIN KING: Then I will defy you!

LITTLEFIELD: That's not enough! Defiance is not enough, mister!

CAPTAIN KING: It's all I've got.

LITTLEFIELD: I expect more of a man than rebellion when his morals are offended! I expect leadership!

CAPTAIN KING: So do I!

LITTLEFIELD: Are you made of tin? Do you have a key in your back? Are you content to march off a cliff?

CAPTAIN KING: That's you!

LITTLEFIELD: What do you believe?

CAPTAIN KING: I'm not interested in philosophy!

LITTLEFIELD: Neither am I! But maybe we should be!

(A standoff.)

You're me. What do you want out of your service?

CAPTAIN KING: Nothing! A pension!

LITTLEFIELD: What's that say?

CAPTAIN KING: I don't care!

LITTLEFIELD: You just like breaking things?

CAPTAIN KING: I'm not the offender here!

LITTLEFIELD: Why do you serve?

CAPTAIN KING: Got to do something!

LITTLEFIELD: What's your purpose?

CAPTAIN KING: To get through the day!

LITTLEFIELD: Come on, Captain! You're not a machine!

CAPTAIN KING: Might as well be.

LITTLEFIELD: Who are you?

CAPTAIN KING: Nobody!

LITTLEFIELD: You must have a dream!

CAPTAIN KING: No, sir! My dream was shot down in Memphis, Tennessee, on April 4, 1968!

LITTLEFIELD: So that's your story.

CAPTAIN KING: I don't have a story!

LITTLEFIELD: Dashed idealist.

CAPTAIN KING: No shortage of those.

LITTLEFIELD: Captain, Martin Luther King's death does not give you permission to lead a cynical life. Nor to mutiny.

CAPTAIN KING: A man has to be cynical to serve at the pleasure of the wind.

LITTLEFIELD: You're on thin ice.

CAPTAIN KING: At least I'm standing on something.

LITTLEFIELD: You are not an officer!

CAPTAIN KING: I am every inch an officer! But I will not play the fool for you!

LITTLEFIELD: What about loyalty?

CAPTAIN KING: Responsibility trumps loyalty!

LITTLEFIELD: Your responsibility's to me!

CAPTAIN KING: What about that young man?

LITTLEFIELD: He's my problem!

CAPTAIN KING: Not anymore.

LITTLEFIELD: As long as I'm in command!

CAPTAIN KING: He's been victimized!

LITTLEFIELD: I'll address it.

CAPTAIN KING: You *are* it!

LITTLEFIELD: I order you to send Private Davis to me.

CAPTAIN KING (*Simultaneously*): No, sir!

LITTLEFIELD *(Simultaneously)*: No, belay that. Strike that order. Are you going to let the fact that I'm human impeach everything I've done? Captain?

CAPTAIN KING: Yes.

LITTLEFIELD: I'm just a man.

CAPTAIN KING: No, sir! You're not just a man! You have set yourself up as a leader of men—

LITTLEFIELD: Captain, can't you . . .

CAPTAIN KING: And your actions have destroyed your ability to lead!

(Pause.)

LITTLEFIELD: Where's the chaplain stand?

CAPTAIN KING: That's another thing.

LITTLEFIELD: He wants me gone?

CAPTAIN KING: He wants your ass, my soul, and the keys to the car.

LITTLEFIELD: What's he going to do?

CAPTAIN KING: I don't know. Maybe nothing, but he's hanging over this whole thing like bad weather.

LITTLEFIELD: I knew he was a goddamn jackal.

CAPTAIN KING: You can't blame him. You played right into his hands. You put him in the game. You gave him the power.

LITTLEFIELD: He doesn't have the power. You do!

CAPTAIN KING: I haven't got shit!

(Littlefield's at sea.)

LITTLEFIELD: My wife. She can't be exposed to this. What if I resign my commission?

CAPTAIN KING: It's too late.

LITTLEFIELD: She's bet the farm on me.

CAPTAIN KING: It's in motion now. Once that man walked into my office, it was too late, sir.

LITTLEFIELD: You don't have to write it up.

CAPTAIN KING: Don't I?

LITTLEFIELD: There's an understanding among officers to protect our own.

CAPTAIN KING: Against gunfire! Against attack! I can't protect you against your own folly, sir.

LITTLEFIELD: Think of yourself then. If you take down your commanding officer—

CAPTAIN KING: There's nothing I can do!

LITTLEFIELD: If you let him come to me—

CAPTAIN KING: Can't do it!

LITTLEFIELD: Nothing's irreversible.

CAPTAIN KING: Until it is. When that boy doesn't get what he wants, he's going to talk. He's going to yell. And why wouldn't he? All of us depend on the right actions of leadership. *(Remembering a fallen comrade)* Especially the ones on the bottom. I should get out of here.

LITTLEFIELD: No. If you're not here when she gets back, it's going to look strange.

CAPTAIN KING: What are you talking about?! You've got to tell her!

LITTLEFIELD: It was a botch. I didn't even do it! It was a moment. For the love of God, man, it happened to me.

CAPTAIN KING: No, sir. You did it.

LITTLEFIELD: I need time to think.

CAPTAIN KING: Tomorrow will be too late. Tomorrow I have to tell that man that if he wants to speak to someone over me it can't be you! I'll have to send him to General Noyes. And once I do that, you'll be dead in the water.

LITTLEFIELD: And so will you!

CAPTAIN KING: That is correct. If you don't deal with this now, *tonight*, TONIGHT, we're both finished. You for what you did, me for destroying a superior officer's career.

LITTLEFIELD: I have three bronze stars and a perfect record!

CAPTAIN KING: I have two bronze stars! And you do not have a perfect record NOW!

LITTLEFIELD: I've saved men's lives in combat! Devoted my life to the corps! Damn near died in Korea! Commanded in Vietnam! I messed up once! Once! In twenty-two years! While trying to do something good for you!

CAPTAIN KING: For me?

LITTLEFIELD: For you.

CAPTAIN KING: Well, you listen to this. You have done nothing but treat me like a black man when all I wanted was to be treated like a man! And when I asked you not to use me as a symbol, you told me that I *was* a symbol, and it was my duty to allow myself to be used! So here I am! Your Executive Officer! And by your own argument, I represent many people, many people, not just myself! And you, sir, represent things beyond yourself also! And must be held to a standard higher than an individual man!

(Unbeknownst to either of them, Margaret walks in. She stands still and quiet.)

I want nothing to do with any of this. The whole thing makes me sick! I know who you are! I know you've done more right than wrong in your life! So you had sex with a girl. These things happen. But that her husband is an enlisted man under your command . . . It's not that you've done such a bad thing. I might've done worse. It's just that it's utterly fatal to the life you're living now.

(*Littlefield sees Margaret. Then King sees her. King explodes in frustration:*)

Goddammit!

(*King storms out without another word. The door slams. Margaret and her husband face each other. After an eternity, he speaks:*)

LITTLEFIELD: Margaret.
MARGARET: What are you going to do?
LITTLEFIELD: Turn myself in.
MARGARET: When?
LITTLEFIELD: Tonight.
MARGARET: Good.

(*Pause.*)

LITTLEFIELD: I just didn't think for a minute, Meg. And I slipped up.
MARGARET: No.
LITTLEFIELD: It's the truth.
MARGARET: No. You never think. You've never thought about any of it.
LITTLEFIELD: You're upset.
MARGARET: You've taken orders all your life, passed them on, but you've never thought.
LITTLEFIELD: That's the military.
MARGARET: You've never known why.
LITTLEFIELD: That's what you do.
MARGARET: Well, is it any wonder, in an unregimented moment on your own two feet that you did something *stupid*?
LITTLEFIELD: Don't talk to me that way!
MARGARET: I'll talk to you!
LITTLEFIELD: Don't make this out to be more than it is.

MARGARET: Thank God Joe got out of here!

LITTLEFIELD: Leave our boy out of this.

MARGARET: Goddamn kindergarten.

LITTLEFIELD: What are you talking about?

MARGARET: You'd kill! You have killed to be a hero. To be admired. My God, should I be surprised about a girl?

LITTLEFIELD: Don't.

MARGARET: And you're still hungry. What did she do? Look up at you?

LITTLEFIELD: I was trying to help!

MARGARET: I should've stopped you years ago.

LITTLEFIELD: This is the only time.

MARGARET: I'm not talking about women! I'm talking about lust! I'm talking about an obscene hunger to be top dog, the king!

LITTLEFIELD: There's nothing wrong with wanting to be great.

MARGARET: Unless you're *not*.

(Pause.)

LITTLEFIELD: You're right. What are we going to do?

MARGARET: There's no "we."

LITTLEFIELD: Don't say that. *(Looks at his watch)* It's getting late. I'd better make that call.

MARGARET: I'll leave you to it.

LITTLEFIELD: No. Could you stand here with me?

MARGARET: I can't.

(He accepts it.)

LITTLEFIELD: I understand.

MARGARET: You're a man. I'll give you that anyway.

LITTLEFIELD: You know, I'm still looking for a good clean fight.

MARGARET: Listen, you dumb son of a bitch: There's no such thing!

(Pause. He thinks this over.)

LITTLEFIELD: You're wrong.

(Pause. She thinks it over.)

MARGARET: Go on. Make the call. *(Sits)*
LITTLEFIELD: What are you doing?
MARGARET: Looking to see.
LITTLEFIELD *(Dials)*: All right. *(Connects)* Hello, it's Lieutenant Colonel Littlefield. I'd like to speak to General Noyes. I'll hold. *(To Meg)* How should I start?
MARGARET: You could tell him to go to hell.
LITTLEFIELD: No. That's kid's stuff.
MARGARET: There it is.
LITTLEFIELD: What?
MARGARET: The diamond in your eye.
LITTLEFIELD *(Into the phone)*: Good evening, sir. I have some bad behavior to report. *(Listens briefly)* Mine.

(The lights fade to black.)

END OF PLAY

p.54

John Patrick Shanley served as a Flame Thrower Gunner in the United States Marine Corps from 1970 to 1972. He never went to Vietnam. He served primarily at Camp Lejeune, North Carolina. Mr. Shanley is interested in your reactions. He can be contacted at shanleysmoney@aol.com.